Protective Intelligence and Threat Assessment Investigations:
A Guide for State and Local Law Enforcement Officials

★ ★ ★ ★

by Robert A. Fein and Bryan Vossekuil

July 1998

Jeremy Travis
Director

Richard Rau
Program Monitor

Robert A. Fein, Ph.D., is a Psychologist for the U.S. Secret Service, U.S. Department of the Treasury. Bryan Vossekuil is Deputy Special Agent in Charge, Intelligence Division, U.S. Secret Service. This project was supported by the National Institute of Justice, Office of Justice Programs, U.S. Department of Justice, under award number 92–IJ–CX–0013, and by the U.S. Secret Service, U.S. Department of the Treasury.

NCJ 170612

Message From the Director, U.S. Secret Service

The U.S. Secret Service is committed to providing a safe environment for each public official it is entrusted to protect. To accomplish this mission, it has developed comprehensive protective programs. The U.S. Secret Service believes that threat assessment and protective intelligence are important aspects of these protection efforts. The purpose of U.S. Secret Service threat assessment and protective intelligence activities is to identify, assess, and manage persons who might pose a threat to those we protect, while the goal of these activities is to prevent assassination attempts.

In carrying out its protective responsibilities, including threat assessment, the U.S. Secret Service works closely with State and local law enforcement agencies. The cooperation, information, and assistance provided through this relationship play a major role in assisting the U.S. Secret Service in fulfilling its responsibilities. At the same time, the U.S. Secret Service has searched for opportunities to further partnerships with State and local police agencies and increase knowledge across all levels of law enforcement.

During the past several years, with the support of the National Institute of Justice and the cooperation of the Federal Bureau of Prisons, the U.S. Secret Service conducted an operational study of the thinking and behavior of the 83 persons known to have attacked or come close to attacking prominent public officials and figures in the United States during the past 50 years. This study, the Exceptional Case Study Project, was recently completed; its findings are leading the U.S. Secret Service to refine and improve its approaches to preventing assassination attempts.

One major product of the Exceptional Case Study Project is this guide, which represents the U.S. Secret Service's efforts to share what it has learned about protective intelligence and threat assessment with State and local law enforcement officials who have responsibilities in the areas of physical protection or protective intelligence.

The U.S. Secret Service is pleased to join the National Institute of Justice in providing this information to our colleagues in the law enforcement and criminal justice communities. We believe that the ideas and information in the guide may assist persons and organizations responsible for preventing attacks on public officials and figures. We also hope that this information will be useful to other individuals and agencies working to prevent other forms of targeted violence, such as stalking, domestic violence, and workplace violence.

Lewis C. Merletti
Director
U.S. Secret Service
U.S. Department of the Treasury

Message From the Director, National Institute of Justice

Throughout our country's history, persons in the public spotlight have faced danger from others. Elected leaders, political figures, educators, musicians, authors—all have been threatened with attacks on their safety and, in some cases, their lives. In the past, often the only courses of action for threatened individuals were to hire private security, to use publicly provided protection (such as the U.S. Secret Service), and simply to be more aware of the dangers facing them.

In recent years, however, efforts have focused on more proactive prevention techniques—developing ways to identify and neutralize people who pose a threat to public officials and figures. The U.S. Secret Service, in its role as protector of the President and other U.S. and international officials, has pioneered these efforts. The U.S. Secret Service developed the field of threat assessment—the process of investigating and analyzing persons and groups who are interested in and capable of attacking public persons—not only to help it fulfill its mission but also to assist other Federal agencies and State and local law enforcement organizations.

Between 1992 and 1997, the U.S. Secret Service, assisted by the Federal Bureau of Prisons, participated in a collaborative project with the National Institute of Justice, studying assassins and would-be assassins of the past 50 years. The purpose of the Exceptional Case Study Project was to examine in detail the lives of assassins and would-be assassins to determine any common traits. Researchers felt that similarities of characteristics, thoughts, or behaviors among past assassins could be key in helping law enforcement officials better identify which persons could pose a present threat to public figures.

This guide is a product of these efforts; project researchers used the data gleaned from the Exceptional Case Study Project to devise a standard set of protocols and procedures for law enforcement and security agencies responsible for protecting public persons and others vulnerable to targeted violence. The guide takes agencies through the entire threat assessment process, from designing a protective intelligence program to investigating suspicious persons to closing a case. The National Institute of Justice and the U.S. Secret Service hope that State and local law enforcement organizations and other criminal justice practitioners will find this guide useful as they work to prevent and deter those who would engage in violence such as stalking, workplace violence, or domestic violence.

Jeremy Travis
Director
National Institute of Justice
U.S. Department of Justice

Acknowledgments

The authors wish to acknowledge the support of the National Institute of Justice, especially the guidance of Richard Rau, Ph.D., and the editorial support of the NIJ publications unit.

Staff from the Federal Bureau of Prisons assisted in obtaining records and interviewing study subjects. The authors especially thank Daniel Cowell, M.D.; Ruth Westrick-Connolly, M.D.; Sally Johnson, M.D.; Casey Skvorc; and staff at the Federal Medical Centers in Rochester, Minnesota, and Butner, North Carolina.

Many persons within the U.S. Secret Service supported the authors' efforts and contributed to the success of the Exceptional Case Study Project (ECSP). The authors especially thank Director Lewis C. Merletti; former Directors John R. Simpson and Eljay Bowron; Assistant Directors H. Terrence Samway, Michael Smelser, David Lee, and Stephen Sergek; Special Agents in Charge Jane Vezeris and Dale Wilson; Deputy Special Agent in Charge James Lucey; Special Agents Marty Allen, Steve Amico, Al Baker, John Berglund, Mike Garduno, Paul Gebicke, and George Sexton; Intelligence Research Specialist Chris Wallace; Research Section Chief Margaret Coggins, Ph.D.; Researchers Angela Macdonald and Joseph Gerston; Senior Intelligence Research Specialist Lynn Zimney; Archivist Michael Sampson; Supervisory Visual Specialist Ed Ross; and Visual Information Specialists Jeff Clemente, Bob Fulk, MacKenzie Kearney, and Patrick Nolan. A special note of thanks is due Assistant Director Sergek, who reviewed ECSP drafts and provided numerous comments.

Pamela Clark Robbins and Henry Steadman, Ph.D., of Policy Research Associates, Inc., provided incisive suggestions and key support at each stage of this project.

Shervert Frazier, M.D., provided invaluable information on violence that shaped the authors' understanding of assassination behaviors.

Gavin de Becker shared information and insights and made many helpful comments about an early draft of the guide.

The authors also wish to thank several other people who reviewed early drafts of the guide, including Randy Borum, Psy.D., Frederick Calhoun, Ph.D., Michael Gelles, Psy.D., Chris Hatcher, Ph.D., Robert Kasdon, Paul Kelly, David Noznesky, Lieutenant Tom Taylor, and Patrick Wolfe. Their comments strengthened the guide.

The authors are grateful to Rita Premo of Aspen Systems Corporation for her editorial assistance.

Finally, the authors wish to acknowledge the contribution of Gwen Holden, who provided both enormous support and great expertise. Her vigorous and skillful editing helped shape the guide into a useful document for Federal, State, and local law enforcement and security professionals.

Contents

CHAPTER 1

Introduction

Threat assessment is a developing field pioneered by the U.S. Department of the Treasury's U.S. Secret Service, which is charged with protecting the President of the United States and other U.S. and foreign leaders. Threat assessment measures involve investigation and analysis of situations and individuals that may pose threats to persons in public life. In 1992, the Secret Service, in partnership with the National Institute of Justice and with assistance from the Federal Bureau of Prisons, began the Exceptional Case Study Project (ECSP), a 5-year study to examine the thinking and behavior of individuals who have attacked or approached to attack prominent public officials or figures in the United States since 1949.[1] ECSP findings reveal general threat assessment information relating to attacks on public officials and figures, while suggesting that broader application of threat assessment protocols by Federal, State, and local law enforcement officials could help anticipate and prevent other crimes, such as stalking and workplace violence.

Drawing from project findings, this guide describes an approach to threat assessment and the protective intelligence investigative process that can be of assistance to Federal, State, and local law enforcement and security professionals with protective intelligence responsibilities. Though not intended to serve as an operations manual, the guide presents information and ideas about developing and implementing protective intelligence programs and activities. Information about the thinking and behavior of persons who have attacked or come close to attacking public officials and figures can help refine law enforcement operations related to preventing and investigating violence and threats of violence.

The Problem

Assassination of political leaders and other public figures has been a significant problem in the United States. Since 1835, 11 attacks on U.S. presidents (4 of them resulting in the death of the President) have occurred. Since 1949, two attacks on Presidential candidates have been attempted, in addition to two attacks on Members of Congress, several assassinations of national political leaders, a number of attacks on State and local elected officials, several murders of Federal and State judges, and several well-publicized attacks on celebrities and business leaders. These attacks do not include many other individuals who presented themselves as warranting serious concern. Each year, Federal, State, and local law enforcement officials and private security officers intercede with thousands of individuals who demonstrate inappropriate or unusual interest in a public official or figure. Some of these individuals were intercepted within lethal range of a target just before they attempted to mount an attack.

Although substantial academic literature on assassination exists, little has been written about the thinking and behavior of assailants who attempt attacks on prominent persons. For example, how do attackers select their targets? What are their motives? How do they plan their attacks? How do these persons assess the security barriers that face them? What communications, if any, do they make before their attacks? To what extent do symptoms of mental illness affect their actions?

Planned, targeted attacks are not confined to those involving prominent public officials and celebrities. Tragically, such attacks are a frequent feature of interpersonal violence in this country today. Cases involving stalking, domestic violence, workplace violence, and bias-motivated criminal activity involve planned—often violent—attacks on intentionally selected targets.

Exceptional Case Study Project

The study examined the thinking and behavior of all 83 persons known to have attacked or approached to attack a prominent public official or figure in the United States from 1949 to 1996. During this time period, 74 attacks and near-lethal approaches occurred.[2] Six attacks were carried out by 16 individuals who were members of groups. Sixty-eight of the attacks and near-lethal approaches were carried out by 67 individuals acting alone. (One individual attacked two public figures.) Targets of these individuals included Presidents, other officials protected by the Secret Service, Members of Congress, Federal judges, prominent national political leaders, State and city officials, business executives, and entertainment, sports, and media celebrities. (See exhibit 1.) All targets were selected because they were prominent persons.

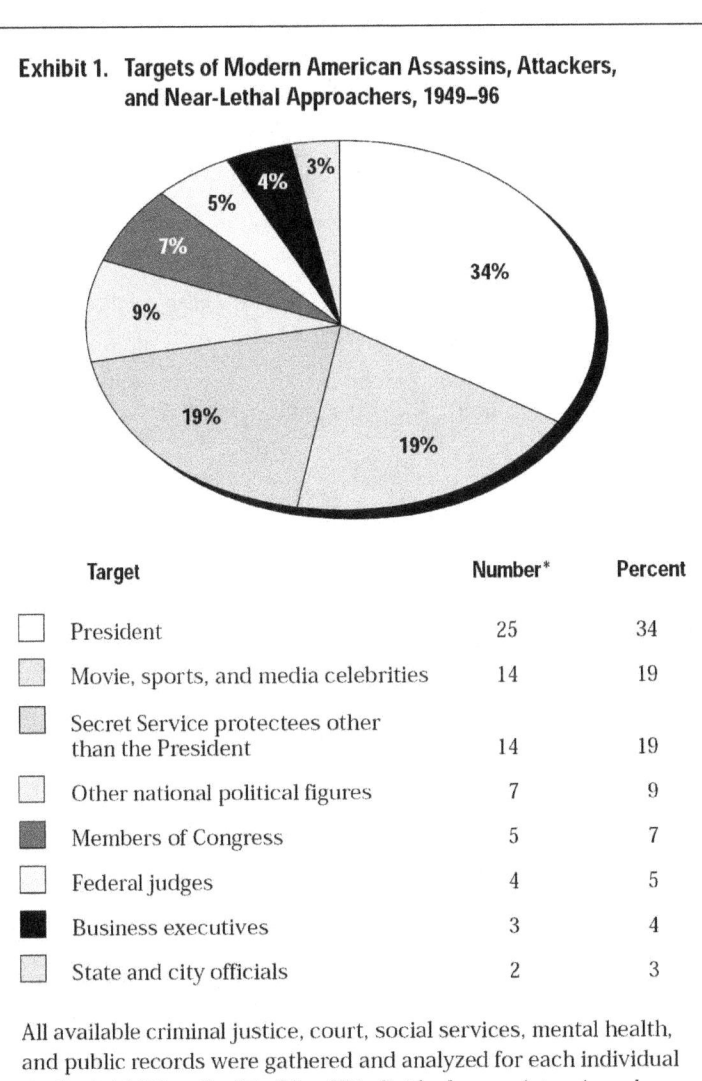

Exhibit 1. Targets of Modern American Assassins, Attackers, and Near-Lethal Approachers, 1949–96

Target	Number*	Percent
President	25	34
Movie, sports, and media celebrities	14	19
Secret Service protectees other than the President	14	19
Other national political figures	7	9
Members of Congress	5	7
Federal judges	4	5
Business executives	3	4
State and city officials	2	3

All available criminal justice, court, social services, mental health, and public records were gathered and analyzed for each individual studied. Additionally, 24 of the 83 individuals were interviewed.

*Note: Total number was 74.

ECSP information gathering and analysis focused on seven major questions:

- How did these individuals develop the idea of assassination, and how did they move from the idea of assassination to lethal or near-lethal action?

- What were the individuals' motives?

- How did the individuals select their targets?

- How did the individuals plan their attacks?

- What communications, if any, did individuals make before their attacks or near-lethal approaches?

- What role, if any, did symptoms of mental illness play in individuals' assassination behaviors?

- Were there key life experiences or incidents that appeared to affect individuals' assassination interests or behaviors?

ECSP findings could be used to help law enforcement and security professionals throughout the United States reevaluate their methods of investigating assassinations and kidnapings, formulating protective strategies, and gathering protective intelligence. This guide describes the following:

- Important information about assassins and assassination behaviors.

- Elements of an effective protective intelligence system.

- Specialized threat assessment investigations.

Threat Assessment Protocols

Law enforcement organizations, private security experts, and the potential targets of violent attacks spend considerable resources on personal protection measures such as enhancements in physical security; 24-hour-a-day physical protection for themselves, their home, and their office; and/or periodic protection. They also may include specialized personal safety training for potential targets.

Threat assessment or protective intelligence is the process of gathering and assessing information about persons who may have the interest, motive, intention, and capability of mounting attacks against public officials and figures. Gauging the potential threat to and vulnerability of a targeted individual is key to preventing violence. Among criminal justice functions, threat assessment holds great promise for determining vulnerability and guiding interventions in potentially lethal situations.

The primary goal of every protective intelligence investigation is to prevent an attack on a potential target. By using a combination of investigative skill, corroboration, and common sense, a protective intelligence investigator can gather the information and evidence to make a thoughtful assessment of the threat an individual may pose to a target. Once an assessment is made, a plan can be developed and implemented to monitor the individual and to intervene, as appropriate, to prevent an attack. Attention to the individual's motives and attack-related behaviors and to the systems (family, work, community, criminal justice, mental health, and social services) that the individual is involved with are key to assessing and managing a potential threat.

Building and maintaining the organizational capacity to conduct protective intelligence investigations at the Federal, State, and local levels takes careful conceptualization, planning, and oversight by experienced law enforcement and security agency managers. Once developed, a protective intelligence program will serve as a key component of a comprehensive protection program to prevent targeted violence.

CHAPTER 2

**Assassins and
Assassination
Behavior**

*T*hree days after a Presidential candidate visited a small Southern city in September 1988, an anonymous letter writer ordered the candidate to drop out of the Presidential race. The letter stated that the writer had attended the candidate's rally with a gun and had stood within shooting range of the candidate. "I didn't shoot this time," said the letter. "I will the next." Enclosed with the letter were three photographs of the rally. Investigative analysis suggested that the photographer was standing within 100 feet of the candidate.

A receptionist in the Governor's office reported that a well-dressed man came to the office, gave his name, and demanded a meeting with the Governor. Asked why he wanted to see the Governor, the man stated, "If he won't meet with me by next Thursday, I will place him under arrest." The man then left the office.

A man called the police to report that a female tenant in his apartment building appeared to be "fixated" on a popular film actor. He said that when he was asked to fix a broken toilet in her apartment about a month ago, he noticed that the walls were covered with posters of the actor. The day before, another tenant had told him that the woman said that "X [the actor] and I will both be dead in a week." When the man read in the newspaper that X was scheduled to make an appearance at a benefit dinner in the city early the following week, he decided to contact the police.

These are examples of situations that come to the attention of Federal, State, and local law enforcement authorities and security managers. Any of these cases may present a risk to a target. The overwhelming majority of cases that come to law enforcement's attention do not result in attacks. But, a few cases do culminate in assassination attempts. Sometimes, individuals and groups attempt assassinations without becoming known to authorities before they attack.

The Assassin

Three prevalent beliefs about assassination exist in popular culture, largely unsupported by data that have been gathered and analyzed about attackers of public officials and figures in the United States. Critical thinking about assassination behaviors proves these beliefs to be myths.

Myth 1:   There is a profile of "the assassin."

Fact: **Attackers and near-lethal approachers do not fit any one descriptive or demographic profile (or even several descriptive or demographic profiles).**

Much has been written about profiles of assassins, but in reality there are no accurate descriptive or demographic profiles of American assassins, attackers, and near-lethal approachers. American assassins and attackers have been both men and women of various ages, educational backgrounds, employment histories, and other demographic and background characteristics.

ECSP findings about the histories and personal characteristics of attackers and near-lethal approachers include the following:

- Their ages ranged between 16 and 73.

- Almost half had attended college or graduate school.

- They often had histories of mobility and transience.

- About two-thirds were described as socially isolated.

- Few had histories of arrests for violent crimes or for crimes that involved weapons.

- Few had been incarcerated in Federal or State prisons before their attack or attempt to attack a public figure.

- Most had histories of weapons use, but few had formal weapons training.

- Many had histories of harassing other persons.

- Most had histories of explosive, angry behavior, but only half of the individuals had histories of physically violent behavior.

- Many had indicated their interest in attacking a public figure to someone else.

- They often had interests in militant or radical ideas and groups, though few had been members of such groups.

- Many had histories of serious depression or despair.

- Many were known to have attempted suicide or to have considered suicide at some point before their attack or near-lethal approach.

- Almost all had histories of grievances and resentments, many directed against a public official or figure.

Although there is no such thing as an assassin profile, potential attackers often engage in many of the same behaviors and actions before their attacks. Mounting an attack on a prominent person requires a number of preparatory decisions and activities— attack-related behaviors. For instance, a potential assassin must choose a target, learn where the target is going to be, choose and secure a weapon, survey security, develop an attack plan, and consider whether and/or how to escape. Although not every ECSP attacker and near-attacker engaged in all of these activities and behaviors, most engaged in several of them.

Myth 2: Assassination is a product of mental illness or derangement.

Fact: Mental illness only rarely plays a key role in assassination behaviors.

Many believe that attacks on public figures are deranged behaviors, without rational or understandable motives; they therefore believe that perpetrators of these crimes must be mentally ill. In most cases, however, mental illness does not appear to be a primary cause of assassination behavior. Attacks on prominent persons are the actions of persons who see assassination as a way to achieve their goals or solve problems, which requires a fairly rational process.

Most near-lethal approachers and the great majority of assassins were not mentally ill—none were models of emotional well-being, but relatively few suffered from serious mental illnesses that caused their attack behaviors.

In almost every case—even those in which the attackers were seriously mentally ill—an attack was a means to achieve an end, such as calling attention to a perceived problem. Moreover, in cases where mental illness clearly played a role in assassination attempts, symptoms of mental illness generally did not prevent the person from engaging in attack-related activities, such as rationally developing an attack strategy. In most situations involving persons with severe and untreated mental illness, the symptoms disable the person's usual problem-solving abilities. However, among mentally ill ECSP attackers and near-lethal approachers, most remained organized and capable of planning and mounting an attack.

Mental health histories of ECSP attackers and near-lethal approachers include the following:

- Many had contact with mental health professionals or care systems at some point in their lives, but few indicated to mental health staff that they were considering an attack on a public official or figure.

- Almost half had histories of delusional ideas, but few of these ideas led directly to a near-lethal approach or attack.

- Few had histories of command hallucinations (imagined voices ordering the individual to take action).

- Relatively few had histories of substance abuse, including alcohol abuse.

Myth 3: **The persons most likely to carry out attacks are those who make direct threats.**

Fact: **Persons who *pose* an actual threat often do not *make* threats, especially direct threats.**

People who study assassination often associate threateners with attackers, as if the two are the same. Many assume that those who *make* threats *pose* real threats. Although some threateners may pose a real threat, usually they do not. However, most importantly, those who *pose* threats frequently *do not make* threats.

- None of the 43 assassins and attackers communicated a direct threat to the target before their attack.

- Fewer than one-tenth of all 83 attackers and near-lethal approachers communicated a direct threat to the target or to a law enforcement agency.

- Two-thirds of the assassins and near-lethal approachers were known to have spoken or written in a manner suggesting that they were considering an attack. Would-be assassins told family members, friends, colleagues, and associates about their thoughts and plans, or they wrote down their ideas in journals or diaries.

These data do not suggest that investigators should ignore threats that are communicated to or about public officials or figures. Many persons may have been prevented or deterred from taking action because of a prompt response to their threatening communications. However, careful attention should also be paid to identifying, investigating, and assessing anyone whose behaviors suggest that he or she might pose threats of violence, even if the individual does not communicate direct threats to a target or to the authorities.

Key Observations on Assassins

Three key observations about assassins and their behaviors emerged from the ECSP study:

- Assassinations and attacks on public officials and figures are the products of understandable and often discernible processes of thinking and behavior.

- Most people who attack others perceive the attack as the means to a goal or a way to solve a problem.

- An individual's motives and selection of a target are directly connected.

Attacks are the product of organized thinking and behavior

Almost without exception, assassinations, attacks, and near-attacks are neither impulsive nor spontaneous acts. The notion of attacking the President does not leap fully formed into the mind of a person standing at a political rally attended by the President. Ideas of assassination develop over weeks, months, even years, and are stimulated by television and newspaper images, movies, and books. Potential assassins seek out historical information about assassination, the lives of attackers, and the protectors of their targets. They may deliberate about which target—and sometimes targets—to choose. They also may transfer their interest from one target to another.

After selecting a target, attackers and near-lethal approachers develop plans and sometimes rehearse before mounting an attack. Often, their days are shaped by their planning activities: What kind of weapon shall I use? Where will the target be? How will I get close? What should I wear? What should I carry with me? Should I leave a letter in case I am killed? For some would-be attackers, such thinking dominates their lives, providing a sense of meaning or a goal that will end their emotional pain.

Frequently, thinking about assassination is compartmentalized; some potential assassins engage in ongoing internal discussions about attacks while maintaining outward appearances of normality. In every ECSP case, assassination was the result of an understandable and often identifiable process involving the attacker's pattern of thoughts, decisions, behaviors, and actions that preceded the attack.

Attacks are the means to a goal

Most people who attack others consider violence the means to a goal or a way to solve a problem. The problem may be that the potential perpetrator feels unbearably unhappy, enraged, overwhelmed, or bereft. If the person views violence as an acceptable or permissible solution, the risk of violent action increases.

Violence—especially assassination—is an event in which a *person*, triggered by an *event* or change, and operating in a *situation* that facilitates, permits, or does not prevent violence, takes action against a designated *target*. These four elements—the potential attacker, event, situation, and target—form the basis for a threat assessment investigation.

The potential attacker. Determining the risk of targeted violence, such as assassinations, begins with gathering information about the potential attacker. In threat investigations and assessments, a key concern is how the person has dealt with *unbearable* stress in the past.

People have many options for dealing with stress: resting, working, exercising, sleeping, changing activities, seeking family support, making contact with friends, etc. However, what happens when the usual means of dealing with stress are not available, do not work, or are not pursued and a person considers life unbearably stressful? At such a time, four reactions are possible. A person might become:

- Physically ill.

- Psychotic or otherwise out of touch with reality.

- Suicidal or self-destructive.

- Violent to others or homicidal.

The event. Investigators should also examine past traumatic events in the life of the individual, particularly those that caused life to seem unbearably stressful. These might include major changes such as:

- Losses of significant relationships (the end of an intimate relationship, death of a parent, or loss of a child).

- Changes in financial status (the loss of a job or threatened financial disaster).

- Changes in living arrangements (being released from an institution, for example).

- Feeling humiliated or being rejected, especially in public.

Major adverse changes in life circumstances, such as losses, fail-ures (real or perceived), and rejections appear to stimulate attack-related behavior—more than half of the ECSP subjects were known to have experienced a major life stressor event in the year before their attack or near-lethal approach.

People deal with life changes and events differently. What might cause one person major worry and distress is met with accep-tance by another. To determine whether an individual may be a cause for concern, three questions must be answered: What events or changes led the individual to perceive life as unbear-ably stressful? How did he or she respond to these events? What is the likelihood that such events or changes will recur in the individual's life?

The situation. The third factor to consider is the individual's specific situation at the time of peak stress. Do people around the person support, permit, or ignore the threat of violence? Do family, friends, colleagues, or supervisors say—directly or indi-rectly—that violence is not a solution to problems and is not permitted? Or is the possibility of violence condoned, accepted, or ignored? People around a person who is acutely at risk of behaving in a violent manner can act to prevent violence.

The target. When conducting a threat assessment, protectors and investigators must also pay attention to the individual's choice of a potential target, assuming the individual has selected a target. The following questions should be addressed:

- How well is the target known to the individual? Is the indi-vidual acquainted with the target's work and lifestyle patterns? Is that information readily available, as in the case of many public officials or highly visible public figures?

- How vulnerable is the target to an attack? What changes in the target's lifestyle or living arrangements could make attack by the individual more difficult or less likely?

- How sophisticated is the target about the need for caution? How concerned about safety is the target? How concerned are those around the target (such as family or staff)? How responsive is the target likely to be to the advice of law enforcement and security professionals?

Motive and target selection are directly connected

Contrary to the general perception, few assassins in the United States—even those targeting major political leaders—have had purely political motives. Other than the Puerto Rican nationalists who attacked President Harry S. Truman in 1950 and Members of Congress in 1954, most recent assassins, attackers, and near-lethal approachers held motives unrelated to politics or political causes. ECSP's examination of the thinking and behavior of the 83 American attackers and near-lethal approachers identified 8 major motives, most of which are personal:

- To achieve notoriety or fame.
- To bring attention to a personal or public problem.
- To avenge a perceived wrong; to retaliate for a perceived injury.
- To end personal pain; to be removed from society; to be killed.
- To save the country or the world; to fix a world problem.
- To develop a special relationship with the target.
- To make money.
- To bring about political change.

Many attackers and near-lethal approachers craved attention and notoriety, while others acted to bring attention to a particular problem. A number of assailants of public officials and figures were consumed with seeking revenge for perceived injuries or harm. A few attacked or nearly attacked public officials or figures in hopes of being killed by law enforcement or being removed from society by being incarcerated. Several believed that assassinating their target was a way to save the world. Others responded to beliefs or imagined voices that they felt ordered them to attack a national leader. A number of subjects approached a celebrity with a weapon to try to force the target into a special relationship. Finally, a few attacked public officials or figures for money, either because they were paid to kill the target or as part of an attempt to secure ransom money.

Targets are selected on the basis of motive, not primarily because of feelings about or hostility toward a particular target or office. Whether an individual likes a particular elected official may be ir-relevant if the individual's motive is to achieve notoriety. "I would have voted for him," said one would-be attacker, "if I hadn't been in jail charged with trying to kill him."

Consistent with their motives, many ECSP attackers and would-be attackers considered more than one target before moving to attack. For example, several individuals whose primary motive was notoriety considered attacking public officials like Governors and Members of Congress before ultimately deciding to attack the President or Vice President; they calculated that an attack on the President or Vice President would receive more attention. Assail-ants often made final decisions about whom to attack because an opportunity for attack presented itself or because they perceived another target was unapproachable.

Who is dangerous?

Not all "dangerous" persons should be considered dangerous to a particular public official or figure. Clearly, a man who is serving multiple life sentences for killing bank customers during a rob-bery is a dangerous person, but he may not pose a threat to a Governor or to an entertainer. Therefore, threat investigators need to consider if he has a motive to attempt such an attack. If he does, the next question is: What is his current and foreseeable ability to attack a Governor or entertainer?

Who, then, is dangerous to public officials and figures? Generally, a person who thinks that attacking a public official or figure is a desirable, acceptable, or potentially effective way to achieve a goal can be considered a potential assassin. If such a person has or develops the capacity to mount an attack on a public official or figure, the threat increases. Changes in thinking about the acceptability or effectiveness of attacking, or changes in ability to attack, may decrease the threat posed.

CHAPTER 3

Elements of a Threat Assessment Program

Effective Design

Designing and implementing a protective intelligence program in a law enforcement or security organization involves two steps. The first step is to define the problem, conceptualize the program and its functions, and establish objectives. The next step is to assess what capabilities are needed to implement the program and to plan so that essential functions can continue over time.

In completing the first step, certain questions must be answered:

- How does the organization define its protective responsibilities? What protective responsibilities does the organization now have? What responsibilities is it likely to have?

- What approaches to protection are currently being used? What kinds of protective services and programs are most likely to fulfill the organization's responsibilities?

- What is the legal basis for protection?

- How often is the organization faced with the task of responding to a threat or a concern about possible violence directed against a public official or figure?

- What currently happens when a threat is received by a protected person's office?

- What should occur when an individual who might be interested in harming a public official or figure comes to attention? For instance, who should be notified?

- Is the organization faced with other targeted violence investigative concerns such as stalking or workplace violence?

Protective services encompass a range of functions, including protective intelligence and physical protection, designed to shield potential targets of violent attacks or assassinations. Visible protectors, such as uniformed officers and security agents, are deployed to defend against any attempted attack on a protected person. Other physical protection measures, such as metal detectors, may keep persons with weapons away from a protected person and deter would-be attackers from trying to approach with a weapon.

Protective intelligence—a less visible aspect of protection—consists of programs and systems aimed at identifying and preventing persons with the means and interest to attack a protected person from getting close enough to mount an attack and, when possible, reducing the likelihood that they would decide to mount an attack. Protective intelligence programs are based on the idea that the risk of violence is minimized if persons with the interest, capacity, and willingness to mount an attack can be identified and rendered harmless before they approach a protected person. This involves three key functions:

- *Identification* of persons who might pose a threat.

- *Assessment* of persons who are identified as a potential threat.

- *Case management* of persons and groups deemed a threat to a protected person.

The second step in developing a threat assessment program involves determining what is needed to complete protective intelligence tasks, examining what is needed to conduct threat assessments, and deciding how to maintain the threat assessment program. Again, several questions must be answered:

- Who will carry out protective intelligence responsibilities? What kind of staffing is needed?

- How will the knowledge and expertise developed by protective intelligence investigators be maintained and shared over time?

- How will new investigators learn, and how will experienced investigators teach?

- What balance of specialized threat assessment expertise and general investigative experience is desirable?

- Can the protective intelligence program build ways to learn from its experiences?

- How will case information be stored and retrieved for individual and aggregated case analysis?

The needs of agencies responsible for protective intelligence mainly depend on their activities. For instance, an organization like the U.S. Secret Service, with responsibility for protecting the President and other national leaders, needs to have the ability to respond immediately to information that a person or group may pose a threat to a protected person. Likewise, a police department in a major city may have a substantial need to fulfill ongoing protective responsibilities as well as intermittent needs to support other targeted violence investigations. A security organization responsible for protecting celebrities may require extensive protective intelligence abilities. Smaller security organizations or those with limited or episodic protective responsibilities may have less extensive needs.

Key Functions of a Protective Intelligence Program

A protective intelligence program involves three key functions: identifying those who might pose a threat, investigating and assessing those individuals, and engaging in case management of those who have been deemed a threat to a protected person.

Identification

Identification is the process by which persons who might present a risk to a public official or figure come to the attention of agencies responsible for protective intelligence.

Some persons self-identify—they call, write, e-mail, or approach a public official or figure or indicate an unusual or inappropriate interest in a person. These individuals often give their names or provide other information that leads to easy identification.

The threatener—someone who communicates a direct, indirect, or conditional threat—is the classic example of a self-identifier. Such a person may threaten for various reasons: to warn of a possible attack, to ask to be stopped, to demand help or attention, to express frustration or anger, or to communicate distress. Threats should always be investigated; even if a threat is not an early warning of attack, making a threat is usually a violation of law, which is a valid reason for opening an investigation.

Other persons self-identify by expressing an inappropriate interest in a public official or figure. They may feel that they have (or should have) a special relationship with the potential target, a unique assignment or role to play, or extraordinary information or expertise that must be shared directly with the public official or figure.

In addition to self-identifying, people also come to the attention of law enforcement by being noticed by others who:

- Recognize that the behavior of the individual is of concern.

- Believe that the individual should be brought to the attention of authorities.

- Understand that authorities want to know about persons who might pose a risk to public officials or figures.

- Know how to contact the proper law enforcement or security organization (or know someone who knows how to contact authorities).

Individuals can be brought to the attention of the authorities by various second parties, including other law enforcement agencies, State agencies, security professionals, family members, neighbors, coworkers, mental health practitioners, and correctional staff. But before this can happen, protective intelligence program staff must decide on identification criteria—which kind of persons the unit wants to be informed about: Those who make threats against a protected person? Those who indicate to others that they are considering an attack on a protected person? Those who demonstrate inappropriate interest in a protected person?

Once identification criteria are determined, decisions must be made about education: Who should be informed about how to report cases of potential concern? What should family members, associates, and staff of a public official or figure know? What should be said to the public about reporting cases of potential concern?

Liaison between protective intelligence agencies and the public is a key function of the identification process. Law enforcement and security agencies will receive information only if the public is aware that they have protective intelligence capacities and know how to contact protective intelligence personnel.

In addition, liaison is important within a given organization and with other organizations. Access to information is increased when the protective intelligence unit previously has engaged in liaison efforts designed to educate organizations and individuals who may have information on potential threats about the mission and functions of the protective intelligence unit. People and organizations with information may be more willing to share information if they are aware of the responsibilities of the protective intelligence unit and if they previously have met or become acquainted with protective intelligence staff. For instance, information from other city agencies about possible threats to the mayor's safety is more likely to come to the police department if staff know that the police department has a protective intelligence capacity. In a corporate environment, reports about persons of possible concern will come more readily to those responsible for an executive protection unit if employees know that the unit exists and how to contact unit staff.

Assessment

After an individual who poses a possible threat to protected persons comes to the attention of agencies responsible for protective intelligence, an initial evaluation is conducted and a decision is made about whether to conduct an investigation. If an investigation is opened, investigators gather information about the individual and then evaluate the information collected to determine whether the individual poses a threat to a protected person. The quality of an assessment is related to both the relevance and the range of information gathered. Key facts of a case should be authenticated and corroborated, with appropriate investigative skepticism about the credibility, accuracy, and veracity of witnesses and informants.

Sources of information. Protective intelligence investigators should make use of all the information available about an individual that will help them answer the fundamental question of threat assessment investigations: Does this subject pose a threat to protected persons? Investigators should emphasize factual data that can be corroborated, rather than the opinions of those who know (or purport to know) the individual.

Sources of information include interviews with the individual and those who have had contact with or appear to have information about the individual (employers, coworkers, neighbors, relatives, associates, caregivers, arresting police officers), records from agencies and institutions that have had contact with the individual, writings by or about the individual, and receipts from the individual's purchases and travels.

A variety of strategies and tools are used in protective intelligence investigations, including interviews; searches of people, residences, automobiles, etc.; background checks; reviews of weapons purchases, credit card purchases, phone records, and travel verifications; and consultations with threat assessment professionals.

The processes of information gathering and evaluation occur simultaneously; they are distinct, but influence each other. Newly developed information affects the ongoing evaluation of the risks an individual poses to protectees. At the same time, the evaluation process may suggest new investigative leads or directions of inquiry.

Case management

When sufficient information is gathered to permit a full evaluation, a decision is made about whether the individual being investigated poses a threat to a protected person. If investigators believe that the individual does not pose a risk, the investigation ends and the case is closed. However, information about closed cases should generally be retained for a period of at least several years. An individual may come to an agency's attention as a potential threat again, in which case information from the previous investigation may be invaluable.

If the individual is deemed a threat, a plan to manage the individual and possible risks is developed and implemented. Such a plan may be as simple as periodically confirming the whereabouts, for example, of an individual confined to a correctional or mental health facility for an extended period of time. A case management plan also may involve a pattern of specified contacts with the individual and others around the individual—such as family members, police officers, coworkers, and caregivers—designed to prevent the individual from approaching a protected person and to decrease the risk of violence posed by the individual. In developing and implementing a case management plan, consultation with threat assessment and other professionals is useful. In all cases, the plan should include informing targets or their designated protectors.

Once developed, a case management plan is implemented until the protective intelligence agency decides that an individual no longer poses a threat of violence. At that point the investigation is concluded and the case is closed.

Functions and Approaches of the Case Investigator

Protective intelligence investigations should be based on three principles—investigative skill, corroboration, and common sense—that guide investigators as they develop and execute protective intelligence operations.

Investigative skill

Protective intelligence investigations should be approached with the inquisitiveness and skepticism that are hallmarks of other investigations. The central goal of a protective intelligence investigation is to determine whether an individual has the motive and means to develop or act on an opportunity to attack a protected person. A primary task of the investigator is to gather information, some of which may later be used as evidence, that can be used to determine whether the individual poses a threat to a protected person.

Corroboration

The second component of protective intelligence work is corroboration. Significant facts of a case, including the statements of an individual who may pose a threat, should be corroborated whenever possible. This means, for example, that a report that the individual traveled to a city on a given date should be viewed skeptically until corroborated; investigators should attempt to secure copies of travel and lodging receipts, statements of credible witnesses who saw the individual, and so on. If the individual is to be interviewed, questions regarding recent activities that would form the basis for corroboration may also help the investigator form a judgment about the accuracy and truthfulness of the information gathered during the interview.

Common sense

Protective intelligence investigations, by their nature, involve considerable discretion and judgment on the part of the investigator. Thus, common sense is necessary. For instance, common sense would indicate that a person who attends three events where a protected person is speaking during a period of several weeks (the last time with a pistol) and who has no plausible explanation for attending these events is a subject for concern— even if no direct threats have been made against the protected person.

Likewise, a man serving multiple life sentences in a maximum-security State prison for murdering three people who writes the Governor saying, "I am committed to killing you by any means necessary," may have motives for writing other than a desire to kill the Governor. Common sense suggests that the letter writer may be a dangerous person. However, common sense also leads an investigator to explore other possible motives that might have led the prisoner to threaten the Governor, such as the wish to secure transfer to another prison or to increase his status in the prison population. After such an inquiry, an investigator is better prepared to conclude whether the letter writer poses a threat to the Governor.

Building a Database and Sharing Information

Information about the persons who are subjects of threat assessment investigations should be organized and maintained in a manner that permits search capabilities, efficient retrieval, and analysis. Some individuals come to the attention of the authorities more than once, sometimes months and even years after the initial investigation was completed and the case closed. In these cases, prompt retrieval of case materials fosters an informed decision of what additional investigation, if any, is needed.

Developing a database also permits later analysis of behavior patterns that come to the attention of threat assessment investigators. A database containing both anecdotal and statistical information about individuals who have been investigated could promote future development of training materials and teaching programs for agencies with protective intelligence and physical protection responsibilities.

Creating a database of threat assessment cases is also useful for interagency cooperation. Attackers and would-be attackers often consider multiple targets, who may live in different jurisdictions with various law enforcement agencies and security organizations responsible for physical protection and protective intelligence. To facilitate the detection of patterns of behavior in known would-be attackers, law enforcement agencies should implement information-sharing programs with other such organizations. Under most circumstances, law enforcement organizations are permitted to share such information. In many cases, law enforcement organizations can receive information, even though they may not provide information to other agencies. Other organizations and individuals often understand these restrictions and may be willing to give information that may help prevent attacks.

CHAPTER 4

**Conducting a
Threat
Assessment
Investigation**

Opening a Case

An individual may come to the attention of protective intelligence professionals after exhibiting inappropriate or unusual interest in a protected person or by threatening a protected person. The information may be general ("I'm going to the State capital to even the score") or specific ("John Smith wrote the mayor's name on a .45 caliber bullet last night"). The person may be acting alone or as part of a group. Sometimes an individual is a person acting alone who becomes a fringe member of an extremist group, using the rhetoric and rationale of "the cause" for personal reasons.

Protective intelligence investigators determine whether the individual is already known to the unit and decide—using criteria identified during the program development phase—whether to initiate an investigation. If so, an investigator is assigned to begin an inquiry.

Inappropriate or unusual interest

Much of the information that initially comes to the attention of protective intelligence professionals appears on the surface to be relatively innocuous. When initial information (provided by either a suspected individual or another person) suggests that the suspected individual has an inappropriate or unusual interest in a protected person, it is reasonable to presume that the individual eventually will be deemed to not pose a threat. The investigator's task is to search for information that rebuts this presumption and suggests that the individual does pose a real threat. Often, a relatively brief investigation will confirm that the individual has neither the interest, motive, nor means to mount an attack against a protected person, thus supporting the presumption that the individual is not a threat.

However, initial information sometimes suggests that the individual already has *taken action* on his or her inappropriate or unusual interest, such as going to the target's home or office or approaching the target in a public place. The combination of *inappropriate or unusual interest* coupled with *actions* based on that interest makes the case more serious.

In even more serious cases, the individual's actions involve weapons-seeking or weapons use. It is then reasonable to presume that the individual poses a real threat. Investigators of these persons should gather information refuting the assumption that the individual poses a threat, if such information is available or exists.

Threats

An individual may come to the attention of authorities after making a threat against a protected person or after being accused of making such a threat. Threats should always be taken seriously and investigated. Although many people who make threats against protected persons do not pose a real threat, some make threats in order to convey a warning that they are prepared to act. These individuals may interpret a lack of investigative interest in their threats as permission or encouragement to mount an attack.

Also, some people make threats against protected persons to signal that they are in danger of losing control and hurting someone. Making a threat is a way for them to get attention (albeit less direct than desirable) from authorities who they believe can prevent them from acting violently. Ignoring these threats might make the individual more desperate, possibly increasing the risk of violence to others, such as family members of the individual.

Occasionally, anonymous threats by phone, letter, or electronic mail come to the attention of law enforcement authorities. Individuals have various motives for communicating anonymous threats. ECSP information suggests that a few attackers and near-lethal approachers of prominent persons who made anonymous threats were trying to warn authorities that they were considering attacks. These individuals were ambivalent about attacking and were communicating with the hope that they might be stopped. Yet they did not want to identify themselves and make it more likely that the attack would be prevented.

Anonymous threats, though rarely acted upon, should be taken seriously and investigated to the fullest extent possible. Specific threats indicating that the threatener has plans to attack or that the threatener may have been in proximity to a protected person should be regarded with special concern.

Investigating a Case

Once a case has been opened, the protective intelligence investigator develops an investigation plan with the primary goal of collecting information and evidence that will help determine whether an individual has the interest, motive, and capacity to mount an attack on a target.

A protective intelligence investigation differs from other kinds of assessments of danger because the goal is to prevent a particular kind of violence: attacks directed against public officials or figures. For example, a parole board may try to assess the likelihood that an inmate, if released, will commit another crime. A mental health professional may attempt to predict whether a mentally ill person is likely to act violently if he or she is not hospitalized. These are different kinds of evaluations than the assessment required in a protective intelligence investigation.

Interviewing the subject

Traditionally, protective intelligence investigators have relied on their interview of the individual who is the focus of a protective intelligence investigation as a key (if not the key) source of information. But this rule is not ironclad—for example, if the subject is known to be a member of a radical or militant group, any interview should be considered only within the context of the overall strategy for investigating the group.

The timing of the interview is often a major question. It usually makes sense to first gather preliminary information about a subject's background and interests before conducting an interview, as background information can guide an investigator during the interview. Such background information may lead the interviewer to areas relevant to whether the person poses a threat to particular targets.

Interviews can provide investigators with valuable information about subjects' thinking, motives for engaging in the behavior that initially brought them to the attention of the authorities, behavior that might be of concern, and leads for further investigation. Interviews may corroborate subjects' statements and be the basis for judging their veracity. Interviews also give subjects the opportunity to tell their personal stories, to be heard, and to reassess and redirect their behavior away from activities that concern investigators.

If at all possible, an interview should be conducted in a subject's "natural environment"—for example, at home—permitting the investigator to observe and gather nonverbal information and evidence that is relevant to the investigation, such as writings, pictures, and weapons that are within sight. Also, the investigator will learn about the subject's overall lifestyle and personality traits.

Investigators must sometimes interview persons who appear to be mentally ill. Such interviews often require special patience. Investigators should remember several basic principles regarding interviews with mentally ill subjects:

- Any subject, including a mentally ill subject, will behave in accord with how he or she perceives reality. Thus, to understand how a mentally ill subject has behaved or may behave in the future, investigators must learn how the person perceives reality. For example, a subject who believes that aliens are controlling his mind and telling him to attack the Governor may feel that he is being forced to stalk the Governor, even though he sees himself as generally law-abiding and knows that attacking the Governor is illegal. An investigator who dismisses this thinking as crazy, concluding that the subject is unlikely to act, and who stops the interview may not explore whether the subject has made efforts to get a weapon or travel to sites where the Governor is likely to be.

- People, including those who are mentally ill, are more likely to reveal their thoughts and actions when treated with respect. Mentally ill subjects who perceive their interviewers as interested in hearing what they have to say are more likely to tell their stories than those who feel humiliated or scorned.

- Someone who is acutely or chronically mentally ill may still be able to think clearly in some areas and to determine whether an investigator is speaking truthfully. Interviewers who use a style that is clear, direct, and nonjudgmental are more likely to solicit useful information than those using an approach in which they pretend to agree with a subject's delusions. An interviewer needs to be an active listener and to communicate a genuine interest in hearing and understanding the subject's story, no matter how outlandish it may seem. However, listening and understanding do not mean agreeing; an investigator should take care not to inadvertently reinforce the views of a delusional subject. Respectful skepticism will elicit more useful information: "I haven't had that experience, but I'm very interested in what you believe."

Although interviews can provide valuable information, relying too heavily on interviews does present problems. The information provided by the subject may be incomplete, misleading, or inaccurate. The interviewer may fail to solicit the information that is most relevant to the protective intelligence strategy called for in the investigation. The interviewee may present different information at different points in time, depending on his or her current circumstances, degree of desperation, mental health treatment, or other factors. In some cases, a subject's mental condition may be worsened by the interview.

Content of a protective intelligence investigation

Protective intelligence investigations differ from many other kinds of investigations in that the ultimate goal of these investigations is to prevent an attack, not to secure an arrest or conviction or to verify facts. Thus, any errors should be made on the side of safety and violence prevention.

Corroborated information and evidence. A primary task of a protective intelligence investigator is to seek and collect information and evidence to corroborate the statements of the subject of the investigation. Corroborated information about the individual's thinking and behavior facilitates assessment of the subject's interests, motives, and capacity to attempt to attack a protected person.

Corroborated evidence is more useful to investigators than subjective information and opinions. For instance, in a more traditional investigation, a detective would not ask a subject's wife, "Do you think he would ever pass a bogus check?" Likewise, asking the relative of a subject or a mental health professional questions such as "Do you think he is the type of person who would try to attack the mayor?" are rarely useful.

Areas of inquiry. A protective intelligence investigation of a subject should seek information in five areas:

The facts of the situation that initially brought the subject to the attention of the authorities. The first area of inquiry concerns how the subject came to the attention of the protective intelligence unit. In cases where the subject went to the mayor's office with "special information only for the mayor that will keep the city safe," the answer is obvious. But other situations may be less clear. For example, a threatening letter from the county jail to a judge signed John Doe, Inmate 502, may have been written by inmate Jones to get Doe into trouble. An anonymous call to the local police by a "concerned citizen" about Mary Smith's disparaging comments about the mayor and her recent purchase of a gun may be from a disgruntled employee who hopes to embarrass her by a visit from law enforcement agents. Providers of information may have multiple motives, and eyewitness accounts of people's behavior are notoriously inaccurate. Protective intelligence investigators should carefully establish the facts of a case to determine if the subject being reported is a victim and if the "informant" is the true threat.

General information about the subject. Three kinds of general information about a subject are gathered in a protective intelligence investigation: identifiers, background information, and information about the subject's current life situation and circumstances.

- **Identifiers.** Identifying information (identifiers) includes the following:
  - ○ Name and aliases.
  - ○ Date of birth.
  - ○ Social security and military identification numbers.
  - ○ Current address.
  - ○ Names and addresses of close relatives.
  - ○ Physical description and current photograph.
  - ○ Handwriting samples.

- **Background information.** Background information includes the following:
  - ○ Education and training.
  - ○ Criminal history.
  - ○ History of violent behavior.
  - ○ Military history.
  - ○ History of expertise with and use of weapons.
  - ○ Marital and relationship history.
  - ○ Employment history.
  - ○ Mental health history (especially involuntary psychiatric commitments, episodes of depression or despair, including suicidal thinking and behavior, and violent behavior while mentally ill).
  - ○ History of grievances.
  - ○ History of harassing others.
  - ○ Interest in extremist ideas or radical groups.
  - ○ Travel history, especially in the previous year.

There are four purposes for gathering background information: to learn about past behaviors, interests, and lifestyles of subjects that may influence their current interests, motives, or capacity to attempt an attack; to develop sources of information, if further inquiry into a subject's life (past and present) is needed; to develop information that could help investigators locate the subjects in the future; and to assist in managing cases that are deemed serious.

- **Current life situation and circumstances.** A third area of general information sought in protective intelligence investigations concerns the current living arrangements and environment of the subject being investigated. Inquiry about a person's current situation is based upon the knowledge that some persons engage in extreme behavior or reach out to law enforcement authorities when they are in transition, in crisis, or in an unstable living situation.

Protective intelligence investigators should consider a number of issues related to a subject's current situation. Is the subject in a stable living situation, with basic needs for food, clothing, shelter, and human contact being met? Is the subject currently employed, and how stable is the subject's employment situation? Is the subject currently or soon likely to be in transition or crisis? For example, has the subject recently left a marriage, job, or community? Will the subject soon be discharged from a correctional or mental health institution? How does the stability of the subject's current living situation compare with past living situations and with the subject's likely living situation in the near future? Does the subject appear to be on a downward course? For example, has the subject recently appeared to be giving up hope, becoming more desperate, losing important contacts and supports, or becoming suicidal? Who is the best source to identify and convey this information?

Information about attack-related behaviors. ECSP examinations of the thinking and behaviors of persons who have attacked or approached to attack prominent persons in the United States suggest that many attacks and near-lethal approaches are preceded by discernible attack-related behavior. This behavior is often observed by people in the subject's life; the protective intelligence investigator who discovers such behavior in a subject will recognize it as a warning sign.

The idea that most assassins and near-lethal approachers engage in similar attack-related behaviors is consistent with an understanding of what is involved in mounting an attack on a protected person. An individual must select a target, locate the target, secure a weapon, travel to the vicinity of the target, and try to thwart whatever security measures are in place. These efforts may provide clues, indicating that the subject being investigated has been planning an attack. Protective intelligence investigators should look for evidence of attack-related behaviors, which can be categorized by whether or not weapons are involved.

Behaviors of concern in a threat assessment include:

- **An interest in assassination.** Manifestations of such an interest include gathering information about murder or assassination, writing to or about assassins, following news accounts of violence directed at public figures, visiting sites connected with assassinations, and emulating assassins.

- **Ideas and plans about attacking a public figure or official.** Evidence that a person has been thinking about or planning an attack may be revealed in comments to others, notes in a diary or journal, recent attention to the activities or travel of a public person, inquiries about law enforcement protective measures, travel patterns, attempts to breach security, or recent efforts to secure a weapon.

- **Communicating an inappropriate interest in a public official or figure, especially comments that express or imply an interest in attacking the person.** ECSP information suggests that attackers and near-lethal approachers rarely communicate direct threats to their targets or to law enforcement agencies, but many communicate information that indicates their intention to harm a target to relatives, coworkers, neighbors, or others.

- **Visiting a site linked to a protectee.** Appearance at an event or site where a public official or figure is, is believed to be, or will be in the future is significant. Visits to these sites, when there is no obvious reason for the subject's appearance there, may be evidence of attack-related behavior.

- **Approaching a protectee.** To attack a protected person, an individual usually must travel to an event or site where the public official or figure is scheduled to be. Information that an individual has approached a target by visiting a site under these circumstances may be cause for concern.

Evidence of attack-related behavior involving a weapon should be taken very seriously by protective intelligence investigators. Of special interest is information about subjects purchasing or otherwise acquiring a weapon around the same time as they develop or hold an inappropriate or unusual interest in a public official or figure. In these circumstances, investigators must determine the intended use of the weapon.

Investigators should presume that an individual who has engaged in attack-related behavior involving a weapon or who has breached security is interested in attacking if given the opportunity. Investigative efforts in such a case should focus on ruling out the possibility of an attack. For example, investigators might establish that the individual had valid reasons, unrelated to a possible attack on a protected person, to carry a weapon or to travel to a certain site.

Motives. A thorough protective intelligence investigation involves careful attention to a subject's motives, because motives may determine whether a public official or figure is being targeted for attack and, if so, which persons are at greatest risk.

As noted in chapter 2, the 83 American assassins and near-lethal approachers studied by ECSP researchers had some combinations of eight motives. However, U.S. Secret Service case experience suggests that the motives of protective intelligence subjects who did *not* engage in near-lethal behavior have included the following:

- Bringing themselves to the attention of persons they perceived to be authorities.

- Instigating their involuntary commitment to a mental health or correctional institution.

- Effecting change in a current living situation viewed as intolerable (for example, to be moved from one prison to another).

- Obtaining help, e.g., being stopped from acting violently.

- Getting someone else in trouble.

- Obtaining attention or notoriety or bringing a concern to public attention.

- Achieving a special relationship with a public official or figure.

- Correcting a perceived wrong.

- Being injured or killed.

An investigator's opinion about the rationality of the subject's motives has no bearing on whether the subject will take action. Because subjects' acts are based on their perceptions of reality, the investigator's views will not determine a subject's future course of conduct. It may not matter whether the motives are illogical or rational, foolish or realistic, self-destructive or in the individual's best interests.

For example, a subject who believes that she is a relative of a public figure and that she has been invited to move into the public figure's residence is unlikely to be dissuaded by an investigator's rational analysis. Such a person is likely to continue to believe that she is related to the public figure despite facts to the contrary. The interviewer's tasks in such a case are to understand how the subject views her situation, not to reinforce any delusional ideas, and to try to gauge what action the subject might take based on her perceptions and beliefs.

The motive of suicide can also be a factor in near-lethal approaches or attacks on public figures and officials. This phenomenon—"suicide by cop"—has received considerable attention in the past 10 years. An individual who wants to die, but is not willing or able to take his or her own life, may believe that instigating gunfire by approaching a protected person with a weapon is a way to get killed.

When coupled with an individual's wish for fame or notoriety, suicide becomes an even more ominous motive. An individual whose motives are notoriety and suicide may consider attacking a political leader, even though he or she has no political interest and no negative feelings about the protected person. The only issue that matters is that the public official is protected by armed law enforcement officers and will be accompanied by news media that will record the assailant's death.

Target selection. Many attackers and near-lethal approachers may consider *several* potential targets and change their primary target several times.

For example, the published diary of Arthur Bremer (who shot Alabama Governor George Wallace in 1972) suggests that his first target was President Richard Nixon. After unsuccessfully attempting to position himself to shoot the President during a trip to Ottawa, Canada, Bremer shifted his interest to Wallace, by then a Presidential candidate. Other near-lethal attackers have shifted from one target to another based on their perception of the importance of a given target. One subject shifted between attacking a Governor, a Senator, and a Presidential candidate, settling on the candidate because he thought a "Presidential candidate is much more powerful."

When gathering information, therefore, investigators should be alert to the possibility that a subject has considered, is simultaneously considering, or might consider in the future a number of public officials or figures as possible targets. Selection of a primary target may depend on many factors, such as the subject's motives, ability to travel, financial situation, and opportunities to approach a target, as well as the perceived importance of, the media attention given to, and the perceived security afforded a target.

CHAPTER 5

Evaluating a Threat Assessment Case

A protective intelligence investigation, at least in part, is an effort to predict specific future violence. Two points about violence prediction are worth consideration. First, violence prediction is conditional—not a yes-no, "this person will be violent or will never be violent" proposition. A prediction of violence is a statement that, given certain circumstances or conditions, a specified risk exists that a particular subject will act violently toward a particular target.

Second, targeted violence is different than other kinds of violence, and attacks on public officials or figures appear to be a specific kind of targeted violence. An attack on a mayor, Governor, or President is a different kind of behavior than an armed robbery, rape, or attack on a roommate. A murder of a celebrity or a business leader is a different kind of violence than a murder of a parent or neighbor. ECSP information about attackers and would-be attackers of prominent persons suggests that some factors that have been seen as general predictors of violence, such as a history of violence, may not specifically predict violence toward a public official or figure.

Principles to Guide a Protective Intelligence Evaluation

After information about a subject has been gathered, this material must be organized and evaluated. A two-stage process is suggested. First, information should be examined for evidence of behavior and conditions that would be consistent with the likelihood of a violent attack on a public person. In the second stage of evaluation, the protective intelligence investigator will determine whether a subject appears to be moving toward an attack and, if so, how rapidly.

Protective intelligence investigators should conduct threat assessments using two principles discussed in chapter 2 as guides:

- Assassination is the result of an understandable and often discernible process of thinking and behavior.

- Assassination stems from an interaction of the potential attacker, event, situation, and target.

Questions to Ask in a Threat Assessment

Investigators should ask a number of questions of both the subject and collateral sources throughout the investigation. The answers to these questions will guide the evaluation:

- What motivated the subject to make the statement or take the action that caused him or her to come to attention?

- What, if anything, has the subject communicated to someone else (target, law enforcement, family, friends, colleagues, associates) or written in a diary or journal concerning his or her intentions?

- Has the subject shown an interest in any of the following?

  ○ Assassins or assassination.

  ○ Weapons (including recent acquisition of a weapon).

  ○ Militant or radical ideas/groups.

  ○ Murders, murderers, mass murderers, and workplace violence and stalking incidents.

- Is there evidence that the subject has engaged in menacing, harassing, and/or stalking-type behaviors? Has the subject engaged in attack-related behaviors? These behaviors combine an inappropriate interest with any of the following:

  ○ Developing an attack idea or plan.

  ○ Approaching, visiting, and/or following the target.

  ○ Approaching, visiting, and/or following the target with a weapon.

  ○ Attempting to circumvent security.

  ○ Assaulting or attempting to assault a target.

- Does the subject have a history of mental illness involving command hallucinations, delusional ideas, feelings of persecution, etc., with indications that the subject has acted on those beliefs?

- How organized is the subject? Does the subject have the ability to plan and execute a violent action against a target?

- Is there evidence that the subject is experiencing desperation and/or despair? Has the subject experienced a recent personal loss and/or loss of status? Is the subject now, or has the subject ever been, suicidal?

- Is the subject's "story" consistent with his or her actions?

- Are those who know the subject concerned that he or she might take action based on inappropriate ideas?

- What factors in the subject's life and/or environment might increase or decrease the likelihood that the subject will attempt to attack a target (or targets)?

In addition, an investigator should address troubling or unresolved issues about a particular case, which could include missing information or new information that might clarify the subject's motives and interests.

Attacks on public officials and figures are rare; all cases that are serious enough to be opened deserve a thorough investigation. Usually, information gathered during the investigation will lead to the conclusion that the subject does not pose a threat. However, sometimes the facts cause the investigator to become concerned about the risk a subject poses. These cases require particularly painstaking investigative efforts and consideration.

In most cases, an investigator should consult with other professionals before drawing a conclusion about whether a subject poses a threat to a public official or figure. Another investigator with protective intelligence experience is often the most effective consultant. However, people with special expertise that might pertain to the facts of a given case can sometimes offer a useful perspective. For example, a mental health professional who has experience assessing mentally ill persons who act violently and who is familiar with the operations of law enforcement agencies could help assess information about a mentally ill subject.

Documenting and keeping a record of the information gathered and evaluated in a protective intelligence investigation is vital. A well-documented record permits others to review the case and offer assistance, and shows that the investigation was performed with care and attention. Also, a carefully documented case file provides baseline information about a subject's thinking and actions at a certain point in time, which can be invaluable if the subject is investigated again or if future investigators need to determine whether the subject has changed thought or behavior patterns.

Protection

Those charged with protection of the targeted public official or figure must be notified about cases of concern, and the information should be incorporated into protection activities. The structure and operations of an organization should determine how threat assessment data are connected to protection activities. For instance, if an organization has one unit responsible for protection and one for threat assessment functions, this often can be accomplished through intramural briefings. Briefing of protectors usually includes a description of a subject's identifiers, behavior, interests, and current location and situation. However, such briefings should be two-way exchanges of information, because protectors often have information that can be important in a protective intelligence investigation as well as in followup investigations used in monitoring the subject.

CHAPTER 6

**Managing a
Protective
Intelligence Case**

In most protective intelligence cases, based on the information gathered, investigators determine that an individual does not pose a risk to a public person. The majority of these cases are closed following the investigation, unless a criminal violation occurred (for example, the subject threatened a public official) or protectors feel that the subject may harm a person other than the original target. If a criminal violation has occurred, the case may be presented to the prosecutor's office for possible charges. If investigators believe that a subject is a threat to an unprotected person, they can attempt to direct the subject to the appropriate resources or otherwise intervene to prevent violence.

When a thorough investigation suggests that the subject has the interest, motive, and ability to attempt an attack on a public official or figure, the investigator's task is to manage the case so that violence does not occur. Successful case management involves considerable time and effort and is composed of two functions: efforts directed at protection (discussed in chapter 5), so that a target is shielded from the potential assailant, and efforts directed at monitoring, controlling, and redirecting the subject.

Monitoring, Controlling, and Redirecting the Subject

The central premise of case management efforts is that violence directed against a protected person is in no one's best interest, including that of the potential assailant. Coordinated, consistent efforts to tell the potential attacker that an attack will not be permitted and that it is not in anyone's best interest to attack can increase the chance that a subject will abandon the idea of assassination.

Unless there is reason to do otherwise, the subject should be made aware of the investigation and told that unacceptable interest in a protected person and unacceptable behavior must change. This message should be communicated to the subject clearly and professionally. However, in certain investigations— for example, those involving a member of a radical or militant group—it may not be appropriate to alert the subject.

Many people considered a threat want attention and will accept ongoing contact with the law enforcement or security organization responsible for protective intelligence. Therefore, the subject should be asked to cooperate with being monitored by the investigator and the law enforcement or security agency. For example, the agency might ask the subject to report all planned travel and to check in with the investigator on a regular basis.

Many subjects see law enforcement officers as important authority figures in their lives. Regular, respectful interviews, in which investigators listen while delivering a consistent, clear message about unacceptable behavior, are key to supporting these subjects as they attempt to change. For a mentally ill subject, simply reinforcing the idea that he or she must remain connected to and cooperative with mental health treatment professionals may be sufficient. Other cases, such as those involving terrorists, call for different strategies.

Effective case management is aided by a systems perspective. That is, investigators should identify existing social systems that might help them manage persons who are potential threats. Social systems that might work cooperatively with the investigator to engage, neutralize, and redirect the potential attacker include the following:

- Criminal justice system (prosecutors, courts, probation officers, correctional officials).

- Health and mental health care organizations (managed care organizations, public mental health agencies, local hospitals).

- Social services organizations.

- Religious organizations to which the subject belongs or in which the subject is interested.

- Community organizations.

- Family and friends.

Ending Monitoring

The purpose of connecting the subject to services and systems that will aid and encourage change is ultimately to enable the investigator to discontinue monitoring. After monitoring is ended and a case is closed, the subject may continue to be involved with service systems that aid successful functioning.

The investigator will be able to end monitoring after performing the following tasks:

- Assessing whether (and to what extent) the subject has changed unacceptable thinking and behavior over time.

- Developing and supporting intervention strategies that encourage and help the subject to change.

Sources of postassessment information

To evaluate changes in behavior, an investigator should develop a baseline of the subject's behaviors of concern and then collect information over time about the subject from multiple and consistent sources. Such a strategy takes into account the likelihood that the living conditions may change, as may the law enforcement or security staff with responsibility for ongoing investigation of the subject.

To permit later comparisons to baseline behavior, the investigator should write detailed descriptions of the subject's initial attack-related behavior and worrisome thinking and actions when he or she was first deemed a threat. A list also should be compiled of persons and organizations who can be contacted at regular intervals for information about the subject's behavior. Collateral-source information can corroborate or clarify information gained directly from interviews with a subject during the case management process. An interview with such a subject might be followed by interviews with others who are in regular contact with the subject to determine whether he or she behaves in a manner consistent with his or her statements to the investigator. For example, a prison inmate who tells an investigator that he is no longer interested in the Governor but who is described by the shift commander on the cell block as being intensely interested each time the Governor appears on the news might be suspect in other comments about his interests and behaviors. Similarly, seeking an opinion from a doctor in a mental health unit who has little contact with a subject about the likelihood that the patient will try to kill the Governor may prove less useful than interviewing a mental health worker who frequently interacts with the patient.

Closing a Case

A protective intelligence investigator can close a case when he or she is able to:

- Articulate why a subject was originally considered to pose a threat.

- Document changes in the subject's thinking and behavior that negate the original concerns.

- Describe why the subject is unlikely to pose a future threat to protected persons.

If postassessment contacts have been made, closing the case involves ensuring that the subject understands that the protective intelligence investigator will initiate no further contact. For some subjects, cessation of contact with the investigator may be a desired goal and a relief; for others, the thought of ending contact with officials who they viewed as helping them may be difficult. In most cases, therefore, it makes sense that discontinuance of contact be gradual, rather than abrupt. Ongoing contact with other organizations, such as mental health or social services agencies, can help these subjects function after their contact with the law enforcement or security organization has ended.

Conclusion

The ECSP has developed knowledge about assassins, attackers, and near-lethal approachers and about other forms of targeted violence. This guide has incorporated this information and is offered as an aid for law enforcement agencies and other organizations to formulate their own processes and protocols for investigating, evaluating, and managing people who are considered threats to public officials and figures.

The ECSP underscores an important point: Nearly all citizens of the United States share the task of preventing assassinations and attacks—physical protection and protective intelligence are not just the responsibility of law enforcement and security organizations. The public, other law enforcement and security organizations, mental health and social services agencies, the private sector, and the media can help identify, assess, and manage potential attackers and thus help to prevent attacks and assassinations.

Notes

1. Fein, Robert A., and Bryan Vossekuil, *Preventing Assassination: Secret Service Exceptional Case Study Project,* unpublished report, Washington, D.C.: U.S. Department of Justice, Office of Justice Programs, National Institute of Justice, and U.S. Department of the Treasury, U.S. Secret Service, 1997.

2. A near-lethal approacher is defined here as an individual who exhibits behaviors that suggest he or she is preparing for an attack on another person and who, without intervention, might attack. Such behaviors include acquiring a weapon and traveling to a site where the target is believed to be. An attacker is a person who actually mounts an attack, while an assassin is a successful attacker.

To find out more information about the National Institute of Justice,
please contact:

National Criminal Justice Reference Service
Box 6000
Rockville, MD 20849–6000
800–851–3420
e-mail: askncjrs@ncjrs.org

To obtain an electronic version of this document, access the NIJ Web site
(http://www.ojp.usdoj.gov/nij).
If you have any questions, call or e-mail NCJRS.

About the National Institute of Justice

The National Institute of Justice (NIJ), a component of the Office of Justice Programs, is the research agency of the U.S. Department of Justice. Created by the Omnibus Crime Control and Safe Streets Act of 1968, as amended, NIJ is authorized to support research, evaluation, and demonstration programs, development of technology, and both national and international information dissemination. Specific mandates of the Act direct NIJ to:

- Sponsor special projects and research and development programs that will improve and strengthen the criminal justice system and reduce or prevent crime.

- Conduct national demonstration projects that employ innovative or promising approaches for improving criminal justice.

- Develop new technologies to fight crime and improve criminal justice.

- Evaluate the effectiveness of criminal justice programs and identify programs that promise to be successful if continued or repeated.

- Recommend actions that can be taken by Federal, State, and local governments as well as by private organizations to improve criminal justice.

- Carry out research on criminal behavior.

- Develop new methods of crime prevention and reduction of crime and delinquency.

In recent years, NIJ has greatly expanded its initiatives, the result of the Violent Crime Control and Law Enforcement Act of 1994 (the Crime Act), partnerships with other Federal agencies and private foundations, advances in technology, and a new international focus. Some examples of these new initiatives:

- Exploring key issues in community policing, violence against women, violence within the family, sentencing reforms, and specialized courts such as drug courts.

- Developing dual-use technologies to support national defense and local law enforcement needs.

- Establishing four regional National Law Enforcement and Corrections Technology Centers and a Border Research and Technology Center.

- Strengthening NIJ's links with the international community through participation in the United Nations network of criminological institutes, the U.N. Criminal Justice Information Network, UNOJUST (United Nations Online Justice Clearinghouse), and the NIJ International Center.

- Improving the online capability of NIJ's criminal justice information clearinghouse.

- Establishing the ADAM (Arrestee Drug Abuse Monitoring) program—formerly the Drug Use Forecasting (DUF) program—to increase the number of drug-testing sites and study drug-related crime.

The Institute Director establishes the Institute's objectives, guided by the priorities of the Office of Justice Programs, the Department of Justice, and the needs of the criminal justice field. The Institute actively solicits the views of criminal justice professionals and researchers in the continuing search for answers that inform public policymaking in crime and justice.

www.ingramcontent.com/pod-product-compliance
Lightning Source LLC
Chambersburg PA
CBHW070608290526
45790CB00002B/833